SECRETS OF ANCIENT CIVILIZATIONS

SEARCHING FOR Cleopatra's TOMB

by José Cruz

CAPSTONE PRESS
a capstone imprint

Published by Capstone Press, an imprint of Capstone
1710 Roe Crest Drive, North Mankato, Minnesota 56003
capstonepub.com

Library of Congress Cataloging-in-Publication Data
is available on the Library of Congress website.
ISBN: 9781669087847 (hardcover)
ISBN: 9781669087922 (paperback)
ISBN: 9781669087809 (ebook PDF)

Summary: Cleopatra was one of ancient Egypt's most famous pharaohs. She was also its last. With her defeat and death, Rome finally conquered Egypt and became its new ruler. But nobody knows the location of her final resting place. Learn more about this great queen and how modern science is helping in the search for her long-lost tomb.

Editorial Credits
Editor: Mari Bolte; Designer: Bobbie Nuytten; Media Researcher: Svetlana Zhurkin; Production Specialist: Whitney Schaefer

Image Credits
Alamy: Lebrecht Music & Arts, 9, North Wind Picture Archives, 15, Science History Images, 8; Bridgeman Images: © Look and Learn, 12, 13, 16, Photo © Christie's Images, 27; Dreamstime: David Pillow, 7; Getty Images: AFP/Cris Bouroncle, 19, 21, 24, Edward Gooch Collection, 25; The Metropolitan Museum of Art: Gift of Joseph W. Drexel, 1889, cover (right), 29; Newscom: Barry Iverson Photography, 4, 22, Heritage Images/The Print Collector, 11; Shutterstock: Alejo Bernal (hieroglyphs), cover and throughout, Heracles Kritikos, 23, Ivan Moreno sl, 6, Matyas Rehak, 18, Mia Stendal (light waves), cover and throughout, Moustafa Yehia, 20, Yaroslaff, 5, 30; SuperStock: DeAgostini, 17

Printed and bound in China. PO 6098

TABLE OF CONTENTS

Words in **bold** are in the glossary.

Introduction

A DEEP DIG

A hole yawns open from the sunbaked sand near Alexandria, Egypt. The hole is 43 feet (13.1 meters) deep. It leads to the entrance to an underground tunnel. A team of brave **archaeologists** inch down a rickety ladder. One wrong step could mean death.

A large cemetery near the dig site told scientists an important person was likely buried there.

The tunnel at the bottom was discovered in 2022. It is thousands of feet long. It leads to the Mediterranean Sea. Right now, though, it is filled with foul-smelling water. Dead rats float past the scientists' feet. But they barely notice. They could be seconds away from one of the greatest historical discoveries of all time. They may be about to find the tomb of Cleopatra and Marc Antony.

A coin with Cleopatra's likeness

Chapter 1

ANCIENT EGYPT AT A GLANCE

The period we know as ancient Egypt began around 3100 BCE. That was around 5,000 years ago. During this time, Egypt became unified as a country. The country was led by a king called Narmer, also known as Menes.

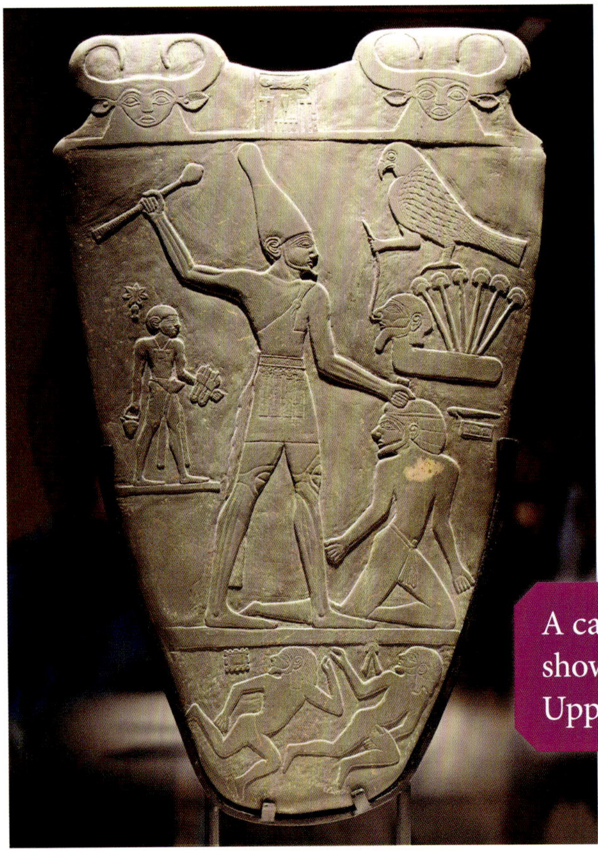

A carved stone tablet shows Narmer uniting Upper and Lower Egypt.

Menes made his capitol near the Nile River. The surrounding Nile River Valley was extremely **fertile**. It was perfect for farming. The rich land meant that Egyptians were able to produce more crops than other countries. Food security meant the population of Egypt could focus its attention on other areas. Egypt soon became known for its powerful military. Its engineers planned huge buildings out of stone. Scholars studied math and literature.

Farmers have grown crops next to the Nile River for centuries.

The Fall of an Empire

During its 3,000 years, Egyptians warred with other civilizations. The Romans **conquered** Egypt in 30 BCE. Around 395 CE, even the great Roman Empire fell. This brought about the end of ancient Egypt. The nation's native religion and language were lost to the sands of time.

One of the great losses of the ancient world was the Library of Alexandria. It was accidentally set ablaze by Julius Caesar in 48 BCE.

What is known about ancient Egypt was learned through **artifacts**. Pieces of history, from small bits of pottery to huge pyramids, reveal much about life during this period. However, finding these clues can be difficult. Historians have been looking for the tombs of two of the most famous leaders, Cleopatra and Marc Antony, for a long time. Modern science has given historians many new tools. Each will help them on their path to solve the mystery of the royals' resting place.

The story of Cleopatra and Antony has inspired many works of art and literature.

Chapter 2

THE QUEEN OF THE NILE

Cleopatra was one of the most beloved rulers of ancient Egypt. She was the last Macedonian queen of Egypt. The Macedonians were an ancient Greek civilization. They conquered Egypt in 332 BCE.

Cleopatra's **regency** began in 51 BCE. She ruled with her two brothers, Ptolemy XIII and Ptolemy XIV. Cleopatra was widely known for her intelligence and charm. She was educated at the Mouseion, a famous school in Alexandria.

Cleopatra's 21-year rule was filled with many triumphs. She managed the construction of temples for both Egyptian and Greek gods. She successfully handled a **famine**, which saved countless lives. She was also the only Macedonian ruler of Egypt to learn the native language of the country.

Cleopatra riding her barge down the Nile River

A Tragic Ending

Around 50 BCE, Cleopatra's brother Ptolemy XIII forced her to flee Egypt. She would not let him turn her out quietly, though. To regain power, she asked the Roman leader Julius Caesar for help. She also met a Roman general named Marc Antony. The two fell in love and married. They spent 11 years living in Rome and Greece.

Marc Antony was a politician and general who served under Julius Caesar.

In Egyptian tales, Isis was a **deity** with magical powers. Cleopatra liked to compare herself to the goddess. Isis was also deeply in love with Osiris, the god of crops. It's possible that Cleopatra thought of Marc Antony as her Osiris. Identifying with deities gave Cleopatra a closer tie to the Egyptian people.

For years after their death, artists imagined Cleopatra as Isis and Antony as Osiris.

Cleopatra encouraged people in Rome to worship Isis. She hoped that she and Antony could unite and rule over their two countries. They would be like Isis and Osiris, who ruled Egypt together.

After the death of Julius Caesar, Antony took his place. Rumors began to spread in Rome about their plans for the Empire. The Romans did not want to be ruled by Cleopatra. The couple fled back to Egypt. However, the Roman army followed.

Cleopatra knew her rule was over. She did not wish to be captured and humiliated by the Romans. When a wounded Antony was brought to her, she made a decision.

FACT

The Roman people did not like Cleopatra's influence on Antony. He already had a Roman wife. Divorcing her made him very unpopular. He also gave Cleopatra land that belonged to Romans.

Roman forces defeated Antony and Cleopatra at the Battle of Actium in 31 BCE.

After Antony's death, Cleopatra put her plan into motion. In life and death, she wished to have Antony at her side. With help from her most faithful servants, she dressed in her most beautiful clothing and prepared for the end. Special instructions were left behind. They said where she and her husband were to be buried. At age 39, she took her own life. It was the final act of the ruler known as the "Queen of the Nile."

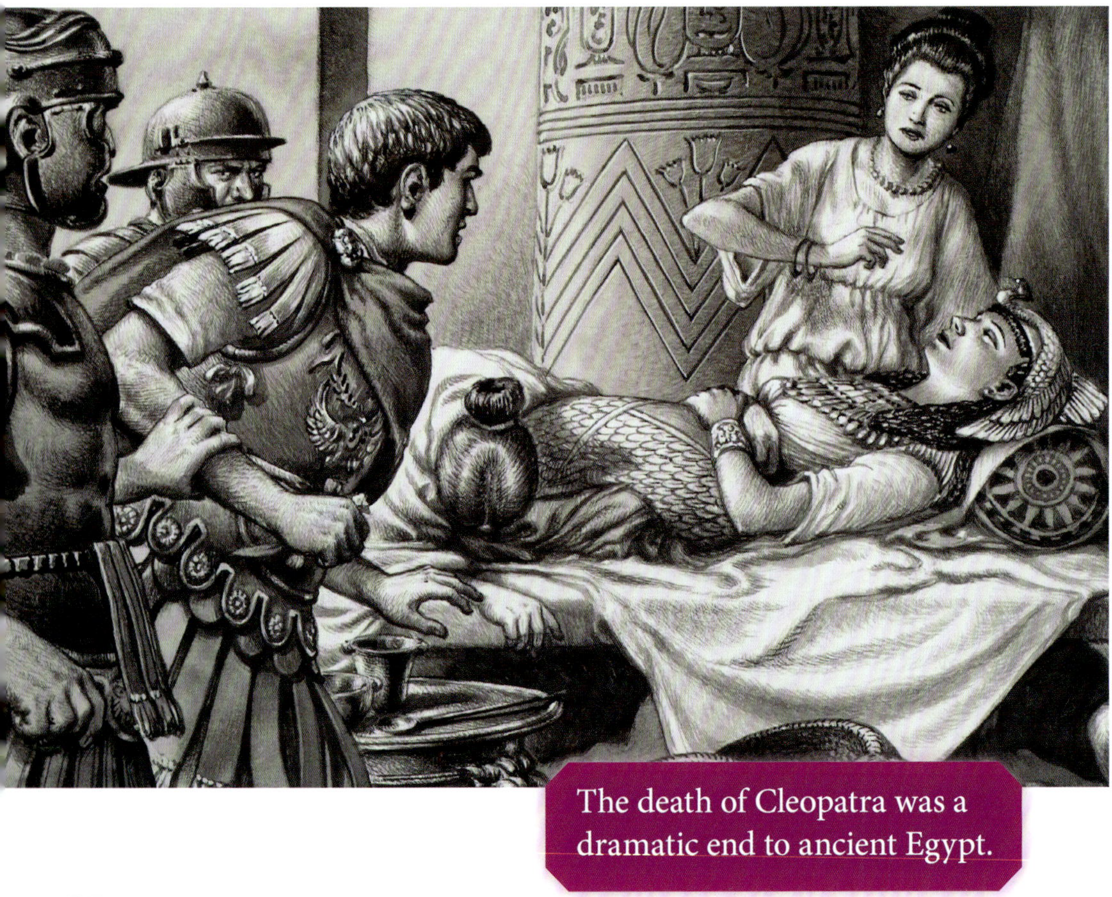

The death of Cleopatra was a dramatic end to ancient Egypt.

A Deadly Bite

Some historians have claimed that Cleopatra poisoned herself by allowing an asp to bite her. Asps were small venomous snakes. It is believed that they were what we call cobras today. However, others believe that Cleopatra used a sharp tool, such as a needle, to poison herself.

Chapter 3

BURIED WITH THE GODS

Legend says that the next Roman leader, Octavian, followed through with Cleopatra's wish. However, no one has ever proved that he did. The tomb's location has been called one of history's greatest mysteries.

No one has ever found the tomb. Archaeologists believe it is somewhere in ancient Alexandria. However, today much of the city's ruins are currently under the Mediterranean Sea.

The deep waters of the Eastern Harbor in present-day Alexandria conceal ancient ruins.

In 2005, Kathleen Martinez left her job as a criminal lawyer to become an archaeologist. The story of Cleopatra inspired Martinez to search for the lost tomb. She examined the quest for Cleopatra's tomb the same way she would approach a legal case. She led an investigation of 21 different potential burial sites. But only one seemed to fit perfectly. It was a temple dedicated to Isis called the Taposiris Magna.

Kathleen Martinez at the Taposiris Magna site

The temple sits on the coast of Egypt. It overlooks where the Nile River meets the Mediterranean Sea. It is the largest temple built for the Egyptian gods Isis and Osiris in the surrounding area. Ptolemy II built it between 280 and 270 BCE. He was one of Cleopatra's ancestors. Martinez, Zahi Hawass, the former Egyptian minister of **antiquities**, and others began a search for Cleopatra and Antony there in 2010.

The name Taposiris Magna means "great tomb of Osiris."

Martinez and her team used ground-penetrating **radar** (GPR) to explore the area before digging. GPR uses radio waves to show what's under the earth's surface. The team also used satellite imagery to find outlines of buried structures. These, and other high-tech tools, helped Martinez's team find statues and jewelry that were 2,000 years old. Coins and figurines had Cleopatra's face on them. There were even 16 mummies.

FACT

Two of the mummies had tongue-shaped **amulets** covered with gold foil. This ensured that they would be able to speak to Orisis, god of the underworld.

Hawass (left) and Martinez with artifacts found at Taposiris Magna in 2009

The discovery of the underground tunnel was announced in 2022. People were excited to hear whether Cleopatra's remains were inside. The tunnel measures 6.5 feet (2 m) tall and 4,300 feet (1,310 m) long. One of the team's greatest difficulties was finding a ladder long enough to reach the bottom.

The tunnel is cut into the underground rock. It is part of a network that leads to other parts of the temple. Some of these areas were totally underwater. Other sections had collapsed. But Martinez planned to keep working. "If there's a one percent chance that the last queen of Egypt could be buried there, it is my duty to search for her," she said.

An alabaster head of Cleopatra was found at Taposiris Magna.

Twin Tunnels

Experts have observed that the tunnel in Alexandria is almost an exact copy of the Tunnel of Eupalinos. This tunnel was an **aqueduct** built in the 6th century BCE on the Greek island of Samos. It was the second tunnel ever fully **excavated**.

TUNNEL OF EUPALINOS

Remains to Be Seen

Some experts have their doubts about the discovery. Hawass is one. He has pointed out that Egyptians typically did not bury their dead inside temples. However, Martinez's mummy discovery already proves that theory wrong.

There could be some debate about Antony's remains as well. The Greek historian Plutarch wrote about great rulers, including Antony. Plutarch stated that Antony was **cremated**.

Zahi Hawass entering a shaft tomb near the temple of Taposiris Magna

Plutarch's biographies focused more on each person's morals and virtues than historical accuracy.

But Plutarch's histories were written more than 100 years after Antony's death. Even Plutarch admitted that it was difficult to determine which events actually happened and which were just stories. The state of Antony's remains is uncertain. Are they mummified or ashes in a jar? The only way to know would be for an archaeological team to find them.

Afterlives of the Rich and Famous

The royalty of ancient Egypt owned many treasures during their lifetimes. They believed that they could take some of these things with them into the afterlife. There are many items archaeologists hope to find when they discover Cleopatra's tomb.

Cleopatra's remains would be the most important. Finding her mummy could answer questions that have stumped people for centuries. Decorations on her tomb walls could show what the pharaoh saw for herself in the afterlife. Historians could finally know her dreams and desires.

Egyptians wanted their dead to have everything they needed in the afterlife. They left food, clothes, furniture, and sometimes even ships and mummified pets inside their burial places. Objects inside Cleopatra's tomb would reveal even more information about the queen.

The tale of Cleopatra has captured the imaginations of people around the world.

THE ONGOING HUNT

Despite the promising discoveries that have been made so far, the hunt for Cleopatra's tomb continues. Questions have been answered, but many more remain.

Fully excavating just the temple could take 40 years. The tunnel would add decades to that. There are no promises that the tunnel holds Cleopatra's tomb—or any tomb at all. Its purpose is still unknown. In the end, it may just be another aqueduct.

As Cleopatra's case shows, even the most important and influential people can become lost to time. Scientists, archaeologists, historians, and other experts are the detectives who seek to rediscover what was lost. Their work ensures that there will always be more to learn about ancient history.

THE QUEEN'S TIMELINE

332 BCE: Macedonia conquers Egypt.

51 BCE: Cleopatra's regency begins.

48 BCE: Julius Caesar arrives in Alexandria.

41 BCE TO 30 BCE: Cleopatra and Antony flee Egypt and live in Greece and Rome.

30 BCE: Death of Cleopatra and Antony; Rome conquers Egypt.

395 CE: Fall of the Roman Empire

GLOSSARY

amulet (AM-yoo-let)—a small charm believed to protect the wearer from harm

antiquities (an-TIK-wuh-tees)—objects used in an earlier time

aqueduct (AK-wuh-duhkt)—a structure that permits water in a canal to flow over a river in its path

archaeologist (ar-kee-AH-luh-jist)—a scientist who studies how people lived in the past

artifact (AR-tuh-fakt)—an object used in the past that was made by people

conquer (KAHNG-kuhr)—to defeat and take control of an enemy

cremate (KREE-mate)—to burn a dead body to ashes

deity (DEE-uh-tee)—a god or goddess

excavate (EK-skuh-vayt)—to dig in the earth

famine (FA-muhn)—a serious shortage of food resulting in widespread hunger and death

fertile (FUHR-tuhl)—good for growing crops

radar (RAY-dahr)—an electronic device that uses radio waves to determine the location of an object

regency (REE-juhn-see)—a period of rule

LEARN MORE

Faust, Daniel R. *The Rise and Fall of Ancient Egypt.* Minneapolis: Bearport Publishing Company, 2025.

Loh-Hagan, Virginia. *Cleopatra.* Ann Arbor, MI: Cherry Lake Publishing Group, 2024.

Britannica Kids: Cleopatra
kids.britannica.com/kids/article/Cleopatra/352970

The British Museum: Ancient Egypt
britishmuseum.org/learn/schools/ages-7-11/ancient-egypt

INDEX

ABOUT THE AUTHOR

José Cruz is an elementary school media specialist based in Southwest Florida. His journalism and short fiction have appeared in print and online, including best-of collections. His favorite topics deal with the dark, the strange, and the mysterious.